Say What You Will

Say What You Will

POEMS BY
Len Krisak

Winner of the 2020 Able Muse Book Award

ABLE MUSE PRESS

Copyright ©2021 by Len Krisak
First published in 2021 by

Able Muse Press

www.ablemusepress.com

Printed in the United States of America

Library of Congress Cataloging-in-Publication Data

Names: Krisak, Len, 1948- author.
Title: Say what you will / poems by Len Krisak.
Description: San Jose, CA: Able Muse Press, 2021. | Series: Able Muse book award for poetry; 10 | "Winner of the 2020 Able Muse Book Award."
Identifiers: LCCN 2020056505 (print) | LCCN 2020056506 (ebook) | ISBN 9781773490908 (paperback) | ISBN 9781773490915 (ebook)
Subjects: LCGFT: Poetry.
Classification: LCC PS3561.R559 S29 2021 (print) | LCC PS3561.R559 (ebook) | DDC 811/.54--dc23
LC record available at https://lccn.loc.gov/2020056505
LC ebook record available at https://lccn.loc.gov/2020056506

Cover image: *Saith the Ancient* by Lady Escabia

Cover & book design by Alexander Pepple

Able Muse Press is an imprint of *Able Muse: A Review of Poetry, Prose & Art*—at www.ablemuse.com

Able Muse Press
467 Saratoga Avenue #602
San Jose, CA 95129

Acknowledgments

I am grateful to the editors of the following journals where many of these poems originally appeared, sometimes in slightly different forms:

Able Muse: "Common"

Adelaide: ". . . But Let It Be. The Buzz of a Cornet"

American Journal of Poetry: "After Callimachus" and "At the Verge"

Apricity Magazine: "Phenomenon"

Chattahoochee Review: "Father and Son Tossing a Football"

Commonweal: "After Charles d'Orléans"

Delmarva Review: "Tiberius"

Dewpoint Literary Journal: "Toy Horse"

First Things: "Deferred" and "Distance Work"

Florida Review: "Ironed, Washed, Folded"

Hudson Review: "March Poem"

Illuminations: "*Woman with a Balance*"

Ithaca Lit: "Boston Subway Ramp, 6 A.M."

The Lyric: "Song"

Measure: "Zeitgebers," "Smoke," "The Eel," "On Learning That Margaret Hamilton Summered for Forty Years on Cape Island, Boothbay Harbor, Maine"

National Review: "The Books" and "Percentages"

New Criterion: "Twenty"

New Delta Review: "In Petrovsky Park"

North of Oxford: "Mourners' Candle" and "Grave"

Other Voices: "Cento: Q & A"

Palette Poetry: "On the Etymology of a Prophylactic Gemstone in a Poem by Elizabeth Bishop"

Pennsylvania Literary Journal: "Salvage"

Plume: "Alimentum" and "Mr. Diana"

PN Review: "Ulysses"

Poet & Critic: "Lower Peninsula"

Raritan: "Ala'llahi al-Mu'tamid on the Guadalquivir: An Anecdote out of Halkin's Biography of Halevi" and "By the Seashore"

The Road Not Taken: "Little Room"

Sewanee Review: "Matter of Time"

Southwest Review: "Sentenced"

Spoke: "Inscription on a Book"

Visions: "Blue Two-Lobed Peanut M & M"

"Tiberius" also appeared in *Poetry Daily*.

Contents

Say What You Will

A Matter of Time

She spies his trench coat first—or rather, sees
It—to the brief exclusion of his hat
And attaché. Who wears a hat these days?
His gait beneath the stately maple trees
Suggests this Asian man's a bureaucrat
Or businessman, content within some maze.
She gazes only long enough to note
He must be sixty if a day, then on
She drives to work herself. But what to think
At five, when there he goes, as if by rote,
Around the blocks—slow ghost that's never gone.
And then it dawns on her. The sidewalks shrink
To aimless tracts of all-day walkabout.
How long, she wonders, till someone finds out?

Ala'llahi al-Mu'tamid on the Guadalquivir: An Anecdote Out of Halkin's Biography of Halevi

The poet-king of old Seville, as he
Went sailing down the royal river, stirred
To what the Andalusian wind was doing:
The waters worked themselves up, knitting waves.
And he, excited by what he could see,
Challenged his courtier (this is what *he* heard):
"*The wind has spun a coat of mail.* Complete
My verse." The man then racked his brain but failed,
While on the banks, among a knot of slaves,
A young girl heard the poet as he sailed.
She called out, in a voice both strong and sweet,
"What splendid armor if it stiffened!" When
The king set out, he'd had no thought of wooing,
But dazzled by her wit, he bought her then
And there, to share, till kingdom come, his life.
No word of future lines; she was his wife.

By the Seashore

translated from the French of Théophile Gautier (1852):
Au bord de la mer

From high up in the air, the moon
Has dropped, from absent-minded hands,
Her glittering fan. It sparkles on
The sea's blue carpet where it lands.

Her silver arm outstretched, she bends
To reach; the fan escapes the try
Her white hand makes as it extends,
Then rides the tide it's carried by.

Moon, I'd dive, though I might drown,
To fetch your fan where men can die,
If from the heavens you'd climb down,
Or I could climb up to the sky!

Alimentum

Birdcage-boned, diminished, frail, and brittle,
　　She lives to finish off what we
Were not permitted to consume when little:
　　Big Macs and Whoppers, preferably
With extra cheese. She bolts—no, *wolfs*—them down,
　　Then begs for pizza, Chinese takeout,
Always up for what we set before
　　Her ninety-year-old appetite.
Deaf as stone, when chauffeured into town,
　　She cases it as if on stakeout,
Scanning fast-food joints for deals . . . for *more*.
　　And though something seems not quite right,
We never do refuse to play along,
　　Give in, or stand amazed—gobsmacked.
Long after *we* have done, *she's* going strong
　　Still. Wings hell-hot; ribs baby-backed;
Burritos, sour cream and guacamole.
　　The way they vanish is unholy,
But what is there to do? A hunger such
　　As hers stands for the will to live,
We're told. But can she need to live too much,
　　Feeding a sibyl's asymptotic
Wasting to a mealy sac of grains?
　　What she demands, we more than give,
Since stopping her would be worse than quixotic.
　　We watch the weight she never gains.
We wait to weigh what makes up her remains.

Mr. Diana

The only bow Diana ever drew
Played second fiddle to his metronomic,
Dance band, front man's wand. One-two, one-two,
It taught me how to cut my time in half,
That tocking-ticking-tocking little stick.
No, fiddling wasn't his métier, but leading
Me through music lessons catatonic.
(Tap-tap, that shrunken-cattail-sized baton
Went glumly indicating down the staff.
When would I get to eighth notes? Someday? Never?)
A cocktail wiener on a small-time skewer,
It filled his hand as if it were his dick,
Saving me from the vices of sight-reading.
One buck a week, my alto sax wheezed on,
Until the day he deemed that I was clever
Enough to huff my way through "Twinkle, Twinkle."
In time, each session's plodding pocks grew fewer
And fewer, to a desultory sprinkle.
"That's all that I can teach you," said Diana,
Leading me from his dubious piano.
I bought a tenor secondhand (the internet)
Last week—as close to him as I've come yet.

Tiberius

There won't be conquests any more.
Time saw to that. Now comes withdrawal.
There's not the slightest chance that war
Will rouse the appetite at all.
Faint images will have to do,
Ghosting memory's blue cave wall.
Bound fast, this is the last Capri
That isolation offers you.
Excite yourself with fantasy
If memory fails. Below, old goat,
The grotto; up above, caprice.
Your vices have you by the throat;
Your organs rot now, piece by piece.
Waves wash the cave and never cease.

After Charles d'Orléans

translated from the French of Charles d'Orléans (ca. 1460):
Le temps a laissié son manteau . . .

The world has thrown its clothes away—
The winter winds, the rain, the cold—
And wears a cloak of sunshine, bold
And clear and shining all the day.

Now every creature's come to say
That new clothes have replaced the old:
The world has thrown its clothes away.
The winter winds, the rain, the cold

Are gone, and every stream must play
In finery the sun's unrolled
With silver sequins, coins of gold.
All waters spangle, ray by ray.
The world has thrown its clothes away.

Sentenced

Halloween yard decoration

The bones have taken up a loafer's slouch,
Lines sprouting from the joints in graceful arcs
That mock the way a corkscrew willow weeps.
They lead to batteries that seem to vouch
For someone's bona fides. Nothing sparks,
Though. This Guignol will give no soul the creeps;
No corpse will die when someone throws the switch.
The Tin Man skullcap's blossomed into wires;
Wags have warned us with "1000 Volts!"
Will any of this scare some shrunken witch
Tonight? Will any children fear the fires
Threatened? No one pauses; no one bolts.
All night, the skeleton prepares to fry—
To frighten small fry with his will to die.
He sits and waits in his electric chair.
The porch lights flicker on. Knock, knock. Who's there?

Father and Son Tossing a Football

To say that they seem distant can't begin
To put it in perspective. Forty yards
Away, the pantomime they're acting in
Features a boy who at each spiral guards
His breast, a man who looks into his hands
The wounded ducks that flutter back in answer.
Despite this play, sometimes the father stands
Stock-still, his progeny become a dancer,
Twisting, then flinching at the catch. His flailing
Annoys the man, who might have been a jock,
And something less than comfortable with failing.
He's slowly getting over any shock,
Though, now resigned to make the most of throwing.
I stand, but do not stand upon my going.

Ulysses

For ten years, locust-suitors were his foemen,
While monster Round-Eye raged to know his nomen,
And killer-wit Odysseus answered "No Man."
Then, like that *pius* one—the Founding Roman—
He spurned his Didos at a goddess' omen
And cleansed his home with blood, blood's perfect bowman.

Twenty

"One buck then would be like ten bucks now."

Doubled over, broken flat, and pressed
In through a slit no one could see, the bill,
Latent behind his Rail Clerks Union card,
Had spent its life in darkness, waiting till
The day he put my loyalty to the test.
Out came Jackson's frozen pompadour,
That gray meringue piled on the hickory-hard
Face; now I was a coconspirator
With someone who had only fathered me
A scant eight years before. His whisper made
A big boy out of me, but even more,
A child of him: "Your mom will never see
This. Just the two of us." Grisaille and jade,
It went back in, its crease a razor blade.

Deferred

I never shot a commie or a Nazi
In '66, but this is what I did:
Fieldstripped an M1 when I was in ROTC.
There were a lot of metal things that slid,
And springs and clips and T-shaped bits galore.
Clip latches, swivels, trigger guard, and trigger
All fell apart. I never went to war.
I think it would have asked for far more rigor
Disassembling my first carburetor.
I learned you never call your piece a gun.
I learned there'd be no sacrifice much greater
Than two semesters' drill with that M1
To get me out of Michigan's PE
Requirement. By April, I was free.

Distance Work

He's rising up like some lone dragon's-teeth-
Sown warrior, or a spiky crocus spear
(Time-lapse-film style). His black sweats form a sheath
As he comes lurching up the shoulder, cresting
Over the hill. At first, it would appear
This training run has been essayed for testing
Some ancient injury. How else explain
His gait? But then I see the rubber tire
He jerks and drags behind him on a chain,
Looking as if he might well soon expire.
And yet, old marathoner that he is,
He lugs on, dropping through my right-side mirror
Etched with that direst of messages
Concerning things that really are much nearer.

After Callimachus

translated from the Greek of Callimachus (ca. 280 BC):
εἰπέ τις, Ἡράκλειτε, τεὸν μόρον ἐς δέ με δάκρυ . . .

When someone, Heraclitus, told me you were dead,
I wept to think how once we talked the sun to bed.
Long, long ago, I fear, your life came to an end.
And you are ashes now, my Halicarnassian friend.
But all your nightingales are living—singing still—
And Hades has not grasped them . . . and he never will.

At the Verge

translated from the Italian of Eugenio Montale (1937):
In limine

Be happy if the breeze that fans the orchard brings
You back the tidal surge of life here—here
Where tangled nets of memories sink
And founder till they drown and die.
Here was no garden, but a place for sacred things.

It isn't flight you hear—some whir that wings have fanned—
But the eternal womb that's stirring as it wakes.
Look at the thing—a crucible—it makes
Itself from out of this deserted coast, this strip of land.

A kind of furor lies behind this cliff-high wall.
You may—perhaps, if you proceed—
Encounter here the phantom that will save you.
Here is where histories come together, every deed
Rescinded by the future's endgame—all.

Look for some weak place in the net, where cords have burst,
Loosening the stranglehold they have us in. Leap free!
Go! I have prayed that you might have this. Now my thirst
Will ease, my bitter rancor lose intensity . . .

Zeitgebers

Demanding when her breakfast will be ready
(It's nine p.m., with dinner barely done),
She shuffles out her bedroom door, unsteady
But determined to inspect the sun.
We guide her to the locked front door, so she
Can see, when we have thrown it open wide,
Night's silver asters, clear as they can be,
And constituting proof we haven't lied.
But though the black sky plainly should convince,
She's seized up standing there, her far-off gaze
Not yet attended by that sudden wince
That means she knows these lights are not the day's.
Then back to bed, in blank bewilderment
At how she could have missed the sun's descent.

Smoke

translated from the French of Théophile Gautier (1852):
Fumée

Down there, under sheltering trees:
A hunchbacked hovel of the poor—
Walls crumbling, roof down on its knees.
Moss blots the threshold of the door.

The window's shutter is its mouth.
But like a tepid winter breath
Exhaled from some living mouth,
This hovel shows it's far from death.

It stands there shabby, closed in, shut.
But smoke is spiraling. A corkscrew's
Thin blue thread curls from that hut:
Its soul, which carries God the news.

The Eel

translated from the Italian of Eugenio Montale (1948):
L'anguilla

The eel, the siren
Of the icy seas, that leaves the Baltic
To reach our seas,
Our rivers, and our estuaries,
Our rivers rising from the deep, below the hostile flood,
From branch on into branch, and then
From capillary on to capillary, growing thin
And ever inward, always more, on through the core
Of rock, still infiltrating on its way
Between the rills of mud, until one day
Light glancing from the chestnut trees
Ignites her fuse in stagnant, standing pools
And in ravines that plunge down from
The ridges of the Apennines, down to Romagna;
Eel, torch, and whip,
Arrow of Love on earth
Which only our arroyos that the sand blows in,
Only our Pyrenean streams, can lead back to
A paradise of fecund generation;
The soul that seeks and searches out
Green life there, there where only
Drought bites, and a mordant desolation,
The sparked scintilla telling us

That everything begins when everything appears
Burnt, charred, and carbonized, a buried stump;
Brief iris, and the twin
To that one which your lashes set, that one
That makes you flash, intact, amid the sons
Of man, and sunk in mud—can't you
Believe she's sister, kin?

On Learning That Margaret Hamilton Summered for Forty Years on Cape Island, Boothbay Harbor, Maine

How far from Hollywood could Margaret get?
Beyond the wand of Billie Burke, whose reach
Could not extend to where the Spinster Bitch
Of Kansas spent each summer. Wicked witch,
You loved land's end—that spit of bouldered "beach"
Where you would sit and watch how suns might set.
As happy as a clam, you hissed at spume
And cackled at the surf, while lobsters red
As rubies screamed that they were melting. Day
By day, sun laid its yellow bricks on bay
And spruce-dark cape; light's poppies bathed your head
In dreams that you might fly night's perfect broom.
Now let the waves slip in, then sleep, my pretty,
Within the lap of time's own emerald city.

Ironed, Washed, Folded

Julie Christie presses on. Her iron will
Still comes down hard on starched white sheets.
Slam and *slam* the heavy thing repeats.
If she can't save the Tsar, her iron will.
Zhivago doctors on; he understands.
The weight of war and love brings down her hands.

*

Religiously, she'd stop there on the brownstone stoop,
He said, before she'd lug the baby carriage in.
Vigilant against the chance of flu or croup,
She'd wash the rubber tires of his pristine pram,
Then pause half up the well-scrubbed steps, half-satisfied,
Before she'd wipe them one more time with germicide.

*

While he lay dying in intensive care,
I stayed with her that week ("to help prepare,"
I said). The night before I left her there,
My clothes all washed (and dried, with sheets of Bounce),
The iron came out—to press my underwear.
My tee shirts needed folding smooth, she said,
Or else they couldn't properly be packed.

The wrinkles flattened as her iron attacked
With hot steam and love's pressing urgency.
It was a medical emergency
Almost.

 The devil's work, she would renounce
With all her strength, with every mortal ounce
She'd need to do the ironing ahead,
Before I flew away and he was dead.

In Petrovsky Park

translated from the Russian of Vladislav Khodasevich (1916):

В Петровском парке

He hung—but wasn't swinging—
By a belt's thin strand.
His hat had fallen off.
It lay black on the sand.
His nails had gouged into
The palm of each clenched hand.

Meanwhile, the sun was rising.
Toward noon, it made its run.
With eyes that were unshut
Before that risen sun,
A man was raised up high—
An elevated one.

His eyes were looking east,
And they were keen, keen, keen.
Below him, those were hushed
Who'd chosen to convene.
And that thin strand of belt
Almost couldn't be seen.

Inscription on a Book

translated from the Russian of Anna Akhmatova (ca. 1959):
Надпись на книге

for Mikhail Lozinsky

From an almost post-Lethean shade,
At that hour when the worlds cave in,
Please accept this gift that's being made—
Small payment for the best gifts that have been.
Do this so that gift, transcending time
And season, indestructible and true—
That lofty freedom of the soul we name
The gift of friendship—as it used to do,
Might smile on me as gently as it did
When it was smiling thirty years ago;
And the Summer Garden fencework grid,
And Leningrad, half-hid in speckled snow,
Might rise, the way there might rise, in this book,
From darkened mists that magic mirrors bring,
And over pensive Lethe's shadowed brook,
The reed that is revived and starts to sing.

Common

Even my enemies by day
      By night will dream—
Impossible as it must seem
    That we should share that way.
This man spewing in my face,
That woman cocked to throw her drink:
    All end up in a place
      Where none may think.

All lie down under cover of
      The darkness shared
By those for whom we never cared
    And those we cannot love.
Deep down my mortal equal lies,
Unconscious in the sleep that knows
    No way to recognize
      That we are foes.

And come that other sleep we call
      A sleep, what then?
Shall I share that with other men
    I cannot bear at all?
Before I dream, I ponder this,
Perhaps preparing to forgive
    Those souls I would not miss.
      I let them live.

Mourners' Candle

The tall glass cylinder wears David's star,
The corpse's body thought of as a wick.
(A flame stands for the soul.) Too weak to char
The flesh, this Hebrew fire flaps at Heaven,
Reminding us that *shiva* translates *seven*.
As it burns, the days are passing quick.
And yet it seems too little and too late
For what its fire would commemorate.
For one brief week, subsiding inch by inch,
The timid blaze is tasteful with respect.
What is it then that makes me want to flinch
Each time I see this flame, to redirect
My gaze? These candles make such meager lamps,
Yet by their light, I see the chimneyed camps.

Grave

While sparse November leaves leave limbs half-flocked,
Earth eats the burden of her dust—a mouth
In which the urn of ash is pocketed.
So taught, I pocket, too, the folded check
That notes how much half of her life was worth.
(Half his as well—her mate much put upon.
Six years now that my father has been gone.)
She left a dirt-floor schoolhouse, barefoot south,
Left there a black sheep brother half-redneck.
She'd plotted from the day she'd given birth,
But never planned this gift her going gave:
Ghiberti's doors and Canaletto's views
Await the sexton's shoveling in the grave,
And it only remains to book the cruise.

Song

The first thin frost
Is clipping afternoon,
And stationery-blue sky has begun
To fade almost to white.
Up high there, in what's left of light,
Bereft of any hint of sun,
All tints will soon be lost.
And yet there's still that towering, tiny moon
In dirty-dime disguise,
The silver-pin jetliner
That begins to rise,
And, sown by some great hand,
A cast of swallows
Growing ever finer
As my failing vision follows
Toward where they mean to land.

The Books

By now, the books have almost filled their shelves
Like some slow love affair reaching its end,
When little space is left for richer selves,
And all have spent the last cent they can spend.

The volumes lined in perfect rows await
A book or two. Then they will be complete,
Standing for hard-won knowledge taken straight
And upright, serving wisdom bound and neat.

Till then, they lean on one another, covers
Touching as they inch on toward the finish.
Who would ever think of books as lovers?
Day by day, the spaces left diminish.

Percentages

He was so certain (says the book)
That when the day was done,
The giant wouldn't be alive.
Why was it, then, that what he took
To fight was not a single stone,
But rather, five?

Cento: Q & A

How can we know the dancer from the dance?
He clasps the crag with crooked hands.
How with this rage shall beauty hold a plea?
It rains into the sea.
Those that I fight I do not hate
(They also serve who only stand and wait,
And still the sea is salt
From stately nave to nave, from vault to vault).
They cannot look in deep.

But I have promises to keep.
I came like water, and like wind I go.
And there was nothing in the town below.
The curfew tolls the knell of parting day.
Nothing gold can stay.

Boston Subway Ramp, 6 A.M.

Discalced, the slipper—hunched and bare and gray—
Took its dominion of the corridor
Deserted but for me. A foot or more
Across, it held its own; it claimed the floor
Of stone. It was the one and only one.
Slip-stepping on, I recognized a nose
And froze, six feet from where this footwear froze.
Buried beneath the city's public park,
Tail questioning, it crouched down on its mark,
Dead set and ready for some starter's gun.
Why should it want to lap the shoddy day
Up with a bloated tongue where it had lain?
I gave the thing a wide berth, passed the bane
That it had not. There was a race to run.

Lower Peninsula

Asked where I'm from,
I say Michigan made me
And touch the birthmark
Below the lifeline
Of my right hand.
Just here, under
The locked knuckles
Of the half-opened,
Half-cupped fist—
A stiff mitten
The map won't fit;
Just here,
Down at the heel
Of the Indian "how"
(A little above
And slightly ahead of
The place where the thickened
Wrist cuts
And twists west).
And though the nuns said
"Thumbs up" in school,
I went ahead
Without a hitch,
And have only to put
My finger on it
To keep my place:
On almost-an-island,
Born with my life
In the palm of my hand.

Blue Two-Lobed Peanut M & M

You've come out all awry, wee thing—
Head nesting-doll-like, podding from
Your body, half askew. How come?
How is it that you couldn't bring
Yourself to see the light—to see
Things whole—and so be wholly formed
To see things through? How could it be
Your sweet thin shell of sugar, warmed
By hand and promised not to melt,
Melts me? Peanut, you've been made blue
By nothing I have done, who felt
Your shell that failed to close up whole,
And left its chocolate to gape
A bit, to show the tender soul
Inside. That you're misshaped, it's true,
Small harmless monster, but you'll do.
And think of what you shall escape:
You shall be served by not being served.
I cradle you. You are preserved.

Salvage

Robed, muled, and hovering curbside over barrel
And bin, what must she think to find so much
With useful life still in it? Fingers peck
And flutter, fidget, snatch. The globe, in peril
Every minute, cries for rescue. Such
A waste. Save, rinse, reuse, repeat—or dreck
Will drown us. What possessed that spendthrift daughter
Of hers, insisting this was hoarding? Earth—
The frail green earth—needs ever-greener care.
Surely that was the baby with the water
In the barrel-bottom, bawling there?
Burdened with what has clearly proved its worth
Throughout the years, she scuffs back up the drive,
Stubbornly cradling all that must survive.

Woman with a Balance

Again the famous, quiet, frame-left light
Blessing all the window will allow:
The balance (delicate, as are the pearls),
The golden coins laid close to hand, the blue
She wears. Deep in the plane, off to her right,
In darkness, a Last Judgment. But for now,
Her face, so maidenly yet not a girl's,
Confirms the careful thought: she knows she, too,
Will find her soul weighed when the bar must lean.
Pulled by the iron judgment of her day,
The pans will fill then, every act unseen
Set in the balance. She can only pray
The thrifty, strict, industrious outweigh
The slothful and the wasteful and not clean.

. . . But Let It Be. The Buzz of a Cornet

translated from the Italian of Eugenio Montale (1937):

. . . ma così sia. Un suono di corneta . . .

. . . but let it be. The buzz of a cornet
Converses with the bees that swarm the oaks.
Inside a shell, the sun begins to set;
A colorful volcano blithely smokes.

And on the desk as well, a coin encased
In lava—shining, weighing down a leaf
Or two. Life, which had seemed so vast
Before, is briefer than your handkerchief.

Toy Horse

As often as I leapt astride
To rowel my sneakers
Into your enameled flanks,
Urging a faster, faster! ride,
I skinned my child-thin shanks.
Your springs—those squeakers
Grown-ups could not abide—
Helped mime that horse-charade.
Mechanically suspended,
I rode till all that ended
And I entered second grade.
Galloping nowhere, memory stirs
To ask me if I ever won my spurs.

Little Room

She had his "Loveliest of trees" by heart,
Though not for what it said, but for its art:
The teasing little math to puzzle out;
The coy, cliff-hanging, snow-for-blossom doubt.
She loved the bride-like cherry's Eastertide,
And how the bloom suggested what had died
Would live again—all this perfected by
The plaintive tone of *rerum lacrimae*.

So when she tendered it in quiet word-
For-word, he took it as he thought that she
Had meant. And he was right.

                      Soon, fifty springs
Will have gone by, and everything he heard
That day will be no more than memory.
(It all depends on how you look at things.)

Phenomenon

Last night I saw the old moon of December—
The Cold Moon—full, with nothing in her arms.
The clouds were sailing all their dark blue forms
Across the sky, and they were massed in number
As they went to see if they would hit
Or miss the old Cold Moon. I stood and saw
Them try to make us three in one dim row,
The moon, the racing clouds, and me. But what
Defied all human sense—that clouds had passed
So near a moon so far—was that they never
Crossed that cold old face. Their floe-thick river
Raced from west to east, but missed, and missed,
And left the Cold Moon distant, full, and free.
And still I do not see how this could be.

On the Etymology of a Prophylactic
Gemstone in a Poem by Elizabeth Bishop

Looking for something, something, she has run
To Rio, a sandpiper in Brazil,
Where drink will type her poem pun by pun.
(Lines bottled up too long pour out until
Beach *grains* of opal flinders flash like *quartz*.)
Poor bird, she can't tell if the tide is higher
Or lower. Booze flows. Sometimes, the verse aborts
Itself; sometimes, she can't tell if it's rye or
Gin that's soaked her in its thwarting mist.
Printing sand in darts, retreats, and darts,
She skitters back and forth to find that stone
Whose power she would dearly make her own.
The quartz grains mix with rose and *amethyst*,
Greek for "not drunk"—the secret, hers alone.

Continuity

Mistakes: how can I tell you what they've meant
To me? For years, I've tracked down shadows, even
In the films of French *auteurs*. They've lent
My life its meaning—all that I believe in.

Not shadows only, either. Clocks—mismatched
From frame to frame—proclaimed the times weren't right,
While props attached came somehow unattached
In later takes. White turned to black; black, white.

Still, errant shadows were my special love.
And when one spoiled some shot, then I was in
A kind of seventh heaven, high above
The cameraman detected by his sin.

The ecstasy of things that could go wrong
Nourished and sustained me through the years,
Propping my spirits up my whole life long.
How strange that failure comforts, warms, and cheers.

Left to myself, I summon shots still rife
With even great directors' careless blunders.
It's lent a special meaning to my life,
Savoring error. I revel in its wonders.

Flood and Tower

The rain is speaking Polyglot
But only has one thing to say.
The sky is so beyond mere gray
You can't tell if it's black or not.
The sky is drilling earth the way
That we were drilled when taught by rote.
Over and over, down and down,
The drops, like tongues, confuse our lot,
Until it seems the earth might drown.
And here we are without a boat.
What is it we are meant to learn?
What have we done? What did we earn?
The rain beats down. What must we do?
The rain would tell us if it knew.

After Housman

Just when it seemed the firmament might fall,
And Earth's foundations shatter into shards,
And there be nothing solid left at all,
Those mocked and taunted by the so-called bards,
Those sneered at for their "blind credulity,"
Stood up and heard their heart's-blood call.
They took scant pay, and saved the clerisy
Of savants and the creatures born to scrawl.
The world had always been but lightly framed,
And was so still when all these fools rebelled . . .
And lost that thing at which they'd aimed.
The scaffolding, defended greatly, held.

Poem for Louise Brooks

Lulu opens up her box;
Dread scatters everywhere, in flocks.
Deadly troubles take off, flying,
And people everywhere start dying.

Louise puts on her bowl of black,
A helmet forged from perfect bangs.
Her smile is staked with gleaming fangs.
Men go for her . . . but don't come back.

Weimar Pandora, Jazz Age vamp:
You sowed the sins of suicide
And murder till you found your Hyde,
Your Ripper, in the London swamp.

Yes, you were beautiful—a face
Not even perfect Garbo had.
Louise, good God but you were bad.
No one will ever take your place.

Auricomous, *Oracle 1966*, 161

Their yearbooks posed them under trees,
With backdrop gothic representing *college*.
They sat sun-dappled, straight-backed but at ease.
Laid in kilt skirts demurely draping knees:
Pale Parmigianino hands. Vague looks
Suggested that they had some sad foreknowledge
Lending a poignance to their doe-soft eyes.
They smiled as they were shot. Some artful books
Beside them were a not uncommon touch
On golf-green grass, and offered viewers hints
That they were scholarly—but not *too* much,
Since even modest stacks could scare away
What classmates thought might be their longed-for prize—
Some square-jawed Deke who stood in for a prince.
Their piercing, placid beauty blessed a day
Written in light that froze their loveliness
In black and white. How could one ever guess
They would achieve their seventies by now?
I'd have them still, if only I knew how.

Metaphor

The poet's truest test, the Stagyrite
Once said, is proving disparates are alike.
A well-known Spaniard had that second sight:
He saw a bull in pieces from a bike

(Its seat the head, its handlebars the horns).
And has *this* ornament that quality—
This wrenched-from-metal magpie that adorns
A neighboring lawn? He speaks out silently,

Squawking from a rust-shut beak of garden
Shears, with forks that serve for feathers,
With trowel feet, and other tools that harden
His stance against the worst of winter weathers.

Himself welded, does this bird bond what's fetched
From far off with what's near, familiar, common?
Do his shovel-breast and wings steel-fletched
Perform the very metaphor they summon?

There are so many like him now, hand wrought
From hammer, lag bolt, chains, and suchlike stuff.
So as to genius, would that Greek have thought
His maker metaphysical enough?

I know that *I* can't say. I only ask
The question, now that I have had my stroll.
I leave to others such a daunting task—
To judge if he has wrought one perfect whole.

Arctic Albatross

The widest wingspan on the earth—
This earth from which their clunky chicks
Will have to launch for all they're worth
The day they stare with eyes that fix
Upon the sea below the cliffs—
Avails them little. Barely fledged,
They will not touch upholding land
For five more years. Each bird that lifts
Off with no surety, that's edged
Up to a lustrum that's been spanned
By millions of its kind for years
That sum to millions, adds its flight
As if there's been no other ever.
Free of this world that it would sever
From its life in atmospheres
Of every lethal weather, might
The albatross, wing-laden, slow,
And awkward on the ground, have chosen
Flight before deck-waddling shame?
Might he have settled on his frozen
Northern skies because below
Lies only more—more of the same
Spoiled world, the same sad, human soil
He leapt from? Maybe. Maybe all
That's left the albatross to care
About comes shooting from the moil
Of water, water everywhere,
And *that* will be his five-year fall—

Downed by a bolt not from that place
Where wedding guest, lord, wright, or miller
Listens to a tale, but by
A sailor's firing up the sky
The arrow of his plunge from grace
To drape the collar of his killer.

From a Line by Bogan

"Another man will tell you what she was."

Now that she's gone, now that she's his,
You have to guess what good she does.
That man can tell you what she is;
This man can tell you what she was:
Root, rain, light, leaf, wind, wave, sun, shade,
The best worst choice he ever made.

Len Krisak graduated from the University of Michigan in 1970 and took his MA from Brandeis University in 1974. In Massachusetts, he worked as a textbook editor and English teacher at Brandeis, Northeastern University, Bentley University, and Stonehill College before retiring in 2010 to write poems and translate.

Also from Able Muse Press

Jacob M. Appel, *The Cynic in Extremis: Poems*

William Baer, *Times Square and Other Stories; New Jersey Noir: A Novel;*
New Jersey Noir (Cape May): A Novel;
New Jersey Noir (Barnegat Light): A Novel

Lee Harlin Bahan, *A Year of Mourning (Petrarch): Translation*

Melissa Balmain, *Walking in on People (Able Muse Book Award for Poetry)*

Ben Berman, *Strange Borderlands: Poems; Figuring in the Figure: Poems*

David Berman, *Progressions of the Mind: Poems*

Lorna Knowles Blake, *Green Hill (Able Muse Book Award for Poetry)*

Michael Cantor, *Life in the Second Circle: Poems*

Catherine Chandler, *Lines of Flight: Poems*

William Conelly, *Uncontested Grounds: Poems*

Maryann Corbett, *Credo for the Checkout Line in Winter: Poems;*
Street View: Poems; In Code: Poems

Will Cordeiro, *Trap Street (Able Muse Book Award for Poetry)*

Brian Culhane, *Remembering Lethe: Poems*

John Philip Drury, *Sea Level Rising: Poems*

Rhina P. Espaillat, *And After All: Poems*

Anna M. Evans, *Under Dark Waters: Surviving the* Titanic*: Poems*

Stephen Gibson, *Frida Kahlo in Fort Lauderdale: Poems*

D. R. Goodman, *Greed: A Confession: Poems*

Carrie Green, *Studies of Familiar Birds: Poems*

Margaret Ann Griffiths, *Grasshopper: The Poetry of M A Griffiths*

Janis Harrington, *How to Cut a Woman in Half: Poems*

Katie Hartsock, *Bed of Impatiens: Poems*

Elise Hempel, *Second Rain: Poems*

Jan D. Hodge, *Taking Shape: Carmina figurata;*
The Bard & Scheherazade Keep Company: Poems

Ellen Kaufman, *House Music: Poems; Double-Parked, with Tosca: Poems*

Len Krisak, *Say What You Will (Able Muse Book Award for Poetry)*

Emily Leithauser, *The Borrowed World (Able Muse Book Award for Poetry)*

Hailey Leithauser, *Saint Worm: Poems*

Carol Light, *Heaven from Steam: Poems*

Kate Light, *Character Shoes: Poems*

April Lindner, *This Bed Our Bodies Shaped: Poems*

Martin McGovern, *Bad Fame: Poems*

Jeredith Merrin, *Cup: Poems*

Richard Moore, *Selected Poems;*
    The Rule That Liberates: An Expanded Edition: Selected Essays

Richard Newman, *All the Wasted Beauty of the World: Poems*

Alfred Nicol, *Animal Psalms: Poems*

Deirdre O'Connor, *The Cupped Field (Able Muse Book Award for Poetry)*

Frank Osen, *Virtue, Big as Sin (Able Muse Book Award for Poetry)*

Alexander Pepple (Editor), *Able Muse Anthology;*
    Able Muse: A Review of Poetry, Prose & Art (semiannual, winter 2010 on)

James Pollock, *Sailing to Babylon: Poems*

Aaron Poochigian, *The Cosmic Purr: Poems; Manhattanite*
    (Able Muse Book Award for Poetry)

Tatiana Forero Puerta, *Cleaning the Ghost Room: Poems*

Jennifer Reeser, *Indigenous: Poems; Strong Feather: Poems*

John Ridland, *Sir Gawain and the Green Knight (Anonymous): Translation;*
    Pearl (Anonymous): Translation

Stephen Scaer, *Pumpkin Chucking: Poems*

Hollis Seamon, *Corporeality: Stories*

Ed Shacklee, *The Blind Loon: A Bestiary*

Carrie Shipers, *Cause for Concern (Able Muse Book Award for Poetry)*

Matthew Buckley Smith, *Dirge for an Imaginary World*
    (Able Muse Book Award for Poetry)

Susan de Sola, *Frozen Charlotte: Poems*

Barbara Ellen Sorensen, *Compositions of the Dead Playing Flutes: Poems*

Rebecca Starks, *Time Is Always Now: Poems; Fetch, Muse: Poems*

Sally Thomas, *Motherland: Poems*

Paulette Demers Turco (Editor), *The Powow River Poets Anthology II*

Rosemerry Wahtola Trommer, *Naked for Tea: Poems*

Wendy Videlock, *Slingshots and Love Plums: Poems;*
    The Dark Gnu and Other Poems; Nevertheless: Poems

Richard Wakefield, *A Vertical Mile: Poems; Terminal Park: Poems*

Gail White, *Asperity Street: Poems*

Chelsea Woodard, *Vellum: Poems*

Rob Wright, *Last Wishes: Poems*

www.ablemusepress.com